✳ **Imagination.**

Beat The Parents

The family quiz book where
kids and parents go head-to-head.

Published and distributed by Imagination,
6161 Santa Monica Boulevard, Suite 100,
Los Angeles CA 90038, USA;
Network House, Bradfield Close, Woking GU22 7RE, UK;
64 North Terrace, Kent Town SA 5067, Australia.
www.imaginationgames.com

First Printing 2008
5 4 3 2 1

Printed in China

ISBN(10) – 1-934524-27-1
ISBN(13) – 978-1-934524-27-5

We would be happy to hear your questions
or comments about this book. Write to:
Imagination, Consumer Advice Department,
64 North Terrace, Kent Town, South Australia, 5067,
Australia or email contactus@imaginationgames.com

Contents

Introduction

It's kids vs. parents in the fun-filled family trivia battle. Parents are asked questions that most kids can answer, and kids are asked questions that most parents can answer.

Bonus rounds can put either team in a winning position. Can the grown-ups measure up to the kids? Or will the kids outdo the parents?

How to Play

Object of the Game
To be the player or team with the most points at the end of the game.

Setting up the Game
Players grab a pen or pencil. If players don't want to mark the book, they can grab some spare paper or write their answers in the notes section found at the back of the book. The game is now ready to begin.

Multi-player Game
Players divide themselves into two teams – KIDS and PARENTS – and work their way through three rounds.

Round One and Two
Each correct answer is worth 1 point. If all questions are answered correctly in a round, 2 bonus points are scored.

Bonus Rounds
Players get the opportunity to gain back any lost points from the previous rounds. The five questions in the Bonus round are worth 3 points each.

Players can increase the pressure by adding a time limit to the Bonus round.

How to Play (continued)

Single-player Game

If you'd like to play a solo game, play for both the parents and kids, correctly answering as many questions as you can. The aim is to beat your personal best.

Winning the Game

At the end of each round, scores are tallied on the Game Total page found at the end of each game. Players or teams compare results – the highest score wins.

Winning teams can proudly display their scores in the Family Hall of Fame. Similarly, losing teams can record their embarrassingly low scores in the Family Hall of Shame. When all games are completed, the winning generation will be revealed!

game one

Turn the page for your first chance to prove that you're boss. Parents, get ready to ask the kids their questions. At the end of each round, check the answers at the bottom of the page, total the score, and see which team won the round.
Let the games begin!

Kids - Round One

Parents, get ready to ask the kids these questions. Each correct answer is worth 1 point. If you get them all right, score a bonus 2 points!

1	True or False? Pineapples grow on trees.	2
2	You have eight cookies and you eat three. How many are left?	2
3	Elvis Presley sang about suede shoes. What color were they?	2
4	Which word is a verb? Whale, wash, when.	2
5	Who was the first man to walk on the moon?	2

☑ for correct answer, ☒ for wrong answer.

SCORE: 2

Answers: 1) False 2) Five 3) Blue 4) Wash 5) Neil Armstrong

Parents - Round One

Kids, ask the parents these five questions. Every correct answer scores
1 point. Get all five right and score a bonus 2 points.

1	What is P. Diddy 's record label: Bad Boy, Bad Dog or Bad Beat?	☑
2	With what would you perform an 'ollie'?	☑
3	What school does Harry Potter go to?	☑
4	What are the two seasons at the Equator?	☑
5	How many signs are there in the Chinese zodiac?	☒

☑ for correct answer, ☒ for wrong answer.

SCORE: 6

Kids - Round Two

Parents, ask the kids these five questions. Every correct answer is worth 1 point. Get them all correct and score 2 bonus points.

1	What is Vincent van Gogh famous for?	✓
2	A banking machine is an A.T.M. What do the initials stand for?	✗
3	What do you call the kitchen on a ship?	✓
4	How many days in a non-leap year?	☐
5	True or False? Your fingerprints were formed before you were born.	✓

✓ for correct answer, ✗ for wrong answer.

SCORE:

Answers: 1) His paintings 2) Automatic Teller Machine 3) Galley 4) 365 5) True

Parents - Round Two

Kids, it's your turn to ask the parents their five questions. Every correct answer is worth 1 point. Get all five right and score a bonus 2 points.

1	How many claws did a Tyrannosaurus have on each hand?	☒
2	What two rivers make up the Nile?	☒
3	What is the nasty white cat in 'Stuart Little' called?	☒
4	Which country eats the most candy per capita: USA, Canada or Denmark?	☒
5	What is Ja Rule's real name?	☒

☑ for correct answer, ☒ for wrong answer.

SCORE:

Answers: 1) Two 2) Blue Nile and White Nile 3) Snowbell 4) Denmark 5) Jeffrey Atkins

Kids - Bonus Round

Okay, kids, it's bonus time. Each correct answer is worth 3 points.
Parents, ask away.

1	What country was Julius Caesar from?	☐
2	How many days are there in January?	☐
3	An Egyptian sphinx had the head of a human and the body of a what?	☐
4	Where does kelp grow?	☐
5	A, E, I and O are vowels. What is the other one?	☐

☑ for correct answer, ☒ for wrong answer.

SCORE:

Answers: 1) Italy 2) 31 3) Lion 4) Underwater 5) U

Parents - Bonus Round

Parents, it's your chance to earn some bonus points. Each correct answer is worth 3 points. Kids, it's your turn to do the asking.

1	Who says: 'To infinity and beyond'?	✓
2	Which are better jumpers: frogs or toads?	✓
3	What powers a 'Wave Blaster'?	✓
4	True or False? There are no spiders on Mount Everest.	✓
5	Who is SpongeBob's grouchy neighbor?	✗

☑ for correct answer, ☒ for wrong answer.

SCORE: 8

Game One - Total

Who will be inducted into the Family Hall of Fame or Shame?
Add up all the rounds and let's find out who the winner is!

Kids
Round One (+ bonus points):
Round Two (+ bonus points):
Bonus round:
Total:

Parents
Round One (+ bonus points):
Round Two (+ bonus points):
Bonus round:
Total:

Write your names where they belong. Will it be the Family Hall of Fame,
or the embarrassing Family Hall of Shame? See pages 174 and 175.

game two

That's the first game down, but there are plenty
of games to go. After each round, check the
answers at the bottom of each page. Good luck.

Kids - Round One

Parents, it's time to see how much the kids know about the older generation. A correct answer scores 1 point, with a bonus 2 points if all answers are correct. Ask away!

1	What records all the flight information on a plane?	☐
2	What is a Greek vase called?	☐
3	What do you call the person who owns property that is rented out to other people?	☐
4	What part of a house has 'eaves'?	☐
5	Which word is a noun? Fork, eat, delicious.	☐

☑ for correct answer, ☒ for wrong answer.

SCORE:

Parents - Round One

Okay, kids, it's your turn to quiz the parents. Let's see how they go with the first five questions. Take it away!

1	How many sides does an ice crystal have?	☑
2	In what country is the original Matterhorn?	☑
3	Who is the main ant in 'A Bug's Life'?	☒
4	What colors are the five Olympic rings?	☒
5	What color is 'Dipsy' the Teletubby?	☑

SCORE:

☑ for correct answer, ☒ for wrong answer.

Answers: 1) Six 2) Switzerland 3) Flik 4) Blue, red, green, yellow and black 5) Green

Kids - Round Two

Here's another chance for the kids to score up to 7 points (if they get all the answers right!). Parents, take it away.

1	What do the letters 'SPF' stand for on suntan lotion?	☐
2	What type of animal is a pachyderm?	☐
3	Finish this well known duo: Tweetie and …	☐
4	If tomorrow is Wednesday, what is today?	☐
5	What is the lookout cage on a pirate ship called?	☐

✓ for correct answer, ☒ for wrong answer.

SCORE:

Parents - Round Two

Okay, kids, let's see how the parents go with the next five questions. Keep score and remember to add 2 bonus points if they deserve them!

1	What is the only mammal that can fly?	☐
2	In which film are Jasper and Horace the crooks?	☐
3	True or False? The North Pole is a huge block of floating ice.	☐
4	What is the name of the old prospector in the movie, 'Toy Story 2'?	☐
5	Name the colors of the rainbow in order.	☐

SCORE:

☑ for correct answer, ☒ for wrong answer.

Kids - Bonus Round

It's bonus time for the kids. Five questions worth 3 points each.
Parents, ask away!

1	In which direction does the Nile River flow?	☐
2	What animal is called 'the ship of the desert'?	☐
3	What is the 'Mona Lisa'?	☐
4	What is ketchup made from?	☐
5	How many wheels does a unicycle have?	☐

☑ for correct answer, ☒ for wrong answer.

SCORE:

Answers: 1) South to North 2) Camel 3) A painting 4) Tomatoes 5) One

Parents - Bonus Round

Okay, kids, it's time for the parents to see how many bonus points they can pick up. The pressure's on - start asking!

1	How long can a snail sleep for?	☐
2	What is the name of Jimmy Neutron's robotic dog?	☐
3	True or False? Children grow faster in springtime.	☐
4	What is the name of the villain in 'The Little Mermaid'?	☐
5	In what movie would you find the evil techno-wizard, 'Fegan Floop'?	☐

☑ for correct answer, ☒ for wrong answer.

SCORE:

Game Two - Total

Who will be inducted into the Family Hall of Fame or Shame?
Add up all the rounds and let's find out who the winner is!

Kids
Round One (+ bonus points):
Round Two (+ bonus points):
Bonus round:
Total:

Parents
Round One (+ bonus points):
Round Two (+ bonus points):
Bonus round:
Total:

Write your names where they belong. Will it be the Family Hall of Fame,
or the embarrassing Family Hall of Shame? See pages 174 and 175.

game three

It's kids questions first so, parents, get ready to ask away. Don't forget to check the answers at the bottom of the page after each round.

Kids - Round One

Okay, parents, let's see how well the kids do with the first five questions. 1 point for each correct answer and 2 bonus points for a perfect round.

1	What color do red and blue make?	☐
2	What country does James Bond spy for?	☐
3	Is a rat a mammal or a reptile?	☐
4	How many hours in a day?	☐
5	True or False? Drinking seawater makes you thirstier.	☐

☑ for correct answer, ☒ for wrong answer.

SCORE:

Answers: 1) Purple 2) England 3) Mammal 4) 24 5) True

Parents - Round One

Another game and another five questions for the parents. Be sure to add their 2 bonus points if they manage to get five correct answers.

1	What is the little girl's name in 'Monsters Inc.'?	☐
2	What can 'Bob the Builder' do: build it, mend it or fix it?	☐
3	What are our four types of taste buds?	☐
4	When Dumbo sneezes, what happens?	☐
5	What is the longest structure ever built ?	☐

SCORE:

☑ for correct answer, ☒ for wrong answer.

Kids - Round Two

Five more questions for the kids. Let's see how well they do this round.
Parents, ask away.

1	What famous tower is the tallest structure in all of Paris, France?	☐
2	What is the yellow part of an egg called?	☐
3	How many foot pedals does a manual car have?	☐
4	What does U.F.O. stand for?	☐
5	True or False? Calcium is found in yogurt.	☐

☑ for correct answer, ☒ for wrong answer.

SCORE:

Answers: 1) The Eiffel Tower 2) Yolk 3) Three 4) Unidentified Flying Object 5) True

Parents - Round Two

Another five questions for the kids to ask the parents. Let's find out just how smart they are.

1	What is the most popular flavor of ice cream?	☐
2	What was the original name of Monopoly's human mascot?	☐
3	What color is Barney the dinosaur?	☐
4	How many types of monkeys are there in the Amazon: 4, 14 or 40?	☐
5	Chinstraps and Gentoos are both types of _____?	☐

SCORE: ☐

☑ for correct answer, ☒ for wrong answer.

Kids - Bonus Round

This is the last chance for the Kids to increase their score. Luckily, each correct answer is worth 3 points. Parents, start asking!

1	Money borrowed to pay off a house is called what?	☐
2	What part of the pig is called its 'trotters'?	☐
3	What type of food is a kiwi?	☐
4	When things go wrong, have they gone hayloft, hay fever or haywire?	☐
5	Who is Kate Hudson's mom?	☐

☑ for correct answer, ☒ for wrong answer.

SCORE:

Answers: 1) Mortgage 2) Its feet 3) Fruit 4) Haywire 5) Actress, Goldie Hawn

Parents - Bonus Round

Kids, it's your turn to quiz the parents in the Bonus round. Let's see how smart they are.

1	What is the capital of Jamaica?	☐
2	In 'Monsters Inc.', what is Sulley's job?	☐
3	What are baby spiders called?	☐
4	In what sport do you load a 'hopper'?	☐
5	Which of the X-Men does Hugh Jackman play?	☐

	SCORE:

☑ for correct answer, ☒ for wrong answer.

Answers: 1) Kingston 2) Scarer 3) Spiderlings 4) Paintball 5) Wolverine

Game Three - Total

Who will be inducted into the Family Hall of Fame or Shame?
Add up all the rounds and let's find out who the winner is!

Kids	Parents
Round One (+ bonus points):	Round One (+ bonus points):
Round Two (+ bonus points):	Round Two (+ bonus points):
Bonus round:	Bonus round:
Total:	Total:

Write your names where they belong. Will it be the Family Hall of Fame,
or the embarrassing Family Hall of Shame? See pages 174 and 175.

game four

Kids, if you don't know the answer, at least
have a guess. You never know - it could pay off.
Here comes game four.

Kids - Round One

Parents, it's another game and another five questions for the kids. Let's find out how smart they are.

1	What number is the Roman numeral 'X'?	☐
2	Is a group of geese a gaggle, a gander or a grouse?	☐
3	What color are emeralds?	☐
4	Where does Santa live?	☐
5	What do you call the man at a wedding who is getting married?	☐

☑ for correct answer, ☒ for wrong answer.

SCORE:

Parents - Round One

Kids, here's the first five questions for the parents. 1 point for each correct answer and 2 bonus points if they get them all right.

1	How long can a flea go without eating: 18 days, 18 weeks or 18 months?	☐
2	Who created the Xbox?	☐
3	In 'Sleeping Beauty', what kind of bush grows around the castle?	☐
4	What color is a Beluga whale?	☐
5	What is the name of the mean girl in 'Rugrats'?	☐

☑ for correct answer, ☒ for wrong answer.

SCORE:

Answers: 1) 18 months 2) Microsoft 3) Briar Rose 4) White 5) Angelica

Kids - Round Two

Take it away, parents, with the next five questions for the kids. 1 point for every correct answer and 2 bonus points for a perfect round.

1	Is a baby whale a kitten, foal or calf?	☐
2	True or False? A tadpole is a baby fish.	☐
3	What band had a drummer named 'Ringo'?	☐
4	What is a 'water closet'?	☐
5	What do you do with a 'javelin'?	☐

☑ for correct answer, ☒ for wrong answer.

SCORE:

Answers: 1) Calf 2) False 3) The Beatles 4) A toilet 5) Throw it - it's a spear

Parents - Round Two

Kids, let's take it away with another five questions for the parents. There's 7 points up for grabs, so start asking!

1	Which holiday has the biggest candy sales : Easter, Halloween or Christmas?	☐
2	What color are Ronald McDonald's shoelaces?	☐
3	How many species of elephant are there in the world today?	☐
4	What are 'bey blades'?	☐
5	What country was 'Mulan' set in?	☐

☑ for correct answer, ☒ for wrong answer.

SCORE:

Answers: 1) Halloween 2) Yellow 3) Three 4) Spinning top toys 5) China

Kids - Bonus Round

Okay, parents, here's five bonus questions for the kids. They'll score 3 points for every correct answer.

1	According to legend, what might you find at the end of a rainbow?	☐
2	Bow-tie, fusilli, and manicotti are all types of what?	☐
3	What is the name of the parasitis fungus that can grow between your toes?	☐
4	Siamese, calico and tabby are all types of what kind of animal?	☐
5	What sort of flying creature is the mythical Pegasus?	☐

☑ for correct answer, ☒ for wrong answer.

SCORE:

Answers: 1) A pot of gold 2) Pasta 3) Tinea pedis, or 'athlete's foot' 4) Cats 5) A horse

Parents - Bonus Round

Only five questions to go and the last chance for the parents to improve their score. Take it away, kids!

1	Pilchard, Muk and Spud are characters on which show?	☐
2	Whose stage name is 'Pink'?	☐
3	Hufflepuff, Ravenclaw and Slytherin are three Hogwarts houses. What is the fourth?	☐
4	Who is the Goddess of Victory otherwise known as?	☐
5	What popular toy was inspired by a bakery pie tin?	☐

SCORE:

☑ for correct answer, ☒ for wrong answer.

1) Bob the Builder 2) Alecia Moore 3) Gryffindor 4) Nike 5) Frisbee

Game Four - Total

Who will be inducted into the Family Hall of Fame or Shame?
Add up all the rounds and let's find out who the winner is!

Kids
Round One (+ bonus points):
Round Two (+ bonus points):
Bonus round:
Total:

Parents
Round One (+ bonus points):
Round Two (+ bonus points):
Bonus round:
Total:

Write your names where they belong. Will it be the Family Hall of Fame,
or the embarrassing Family Hall of Shame? See pages 174 and 175.

game five

Let's get game five underway, and don't forget to add the bonus points if you correctly answer all questions in the round. Good luck to both teams.

Kids - Round One

Here we go again with five questions for the kids. A maximum of 7 points is up for grabs if the kids manage a perfect round, so ask away, parents.

1	What side of the road do the British drive on?	☐
2	Are 'molars' small animals, tropical fruit or teeth?	☐
3	What weapon did knights use for jousting?	☐
4	What is the skin of an orange called?	☐
5	In what country do people wear 'kimonos'?	☐

☑ for correct answer, ☒ for wrong answer.

SCORE:

Answers: 1) The left 2) Teeth 3) A lance 4) Rind 5) Japan

Parents - Round One

Kids, here's five questions for the parents. Let's see how smart they are.

1	A year on Jupiter is equal to how many years on Earth?	☐
2	Which can survive longer without water: a camel, a rat or a reebok?	☐
3	In 'The Flintstones', what kind of dinosaur is Dino?	☐
4	Where was Nicole Kidman born?	☐
5	Was the brain of a Stegosaurus the size of: a walnut, baseball or football?	☐

SCORE:

☑ for correct answer, ☒ for wrong answer.

Kids - Round Two

Parents, it's your turn to ask the kids another five questions.
Let's see how they go this round. Take it away!

1	Which is bigger: the Indian, Atlantic or Pacific Ocean?	☐
2	What is the name of Santa's red-nosed reindeer?	☐
3	Is calico made from cotton, silk or wool?	☐
4	In what city is the 'Acropolis'?	☐
5	True or False? Watermelons grow in water.	☐

☑ for correct answer, ☒ for wrong answer.

SCORE:

Answers: 1) Pacific Ocean 2) Rudolph 3) Cotton 4) Athens, Greece 5) False

Parents - Round Two

Five questions down and here's another five for the kids to ask the parents. Let's see how they go in this round.

1	Which Disney film features a blue fairy?	☐
2	What are comet tails made of?	☐
3	What is the name of the flying game in 'Harry Potter'?	☐
4	What is the primary color of a milk snake?	☐
5	What was Barbie's first movie called?	☐

☑ for correct answer, ☒ for wrong answer.

SCORE:

Answers: 1) Pinocchio 2) Gas and dust particles 3) Quidditch 4) Red 5) The Nutcracker

Kids - Bonus Round

It's make or break time with these five bonus questions for the kids.
Parents, take it away!

1	Was Houdini a juggler, escape artist or tightrope walker?	☐
2	What is a 'Chihuahua'?	☐
3	Everything King Midas touched turned to what?	☐
4	What do the initials D.O.B. stand for?	☐
5	In what sport is there 'love'?	☐

☑ for correct answer, ☒ for wrong answer.

SCORE:

Answers: 1) Escape artist 2) A small dog 3) Gold 4) Date of birth 5) Tennis

Parents - Bonus Round

Kids, here's five bonus questions to ask the parents. Each correct answer is worth 3 points. Let's see how they go!

1	Who wrote 'Yertle the Turtle'?	☐
2	How do emperor penguins keep their eggs warm?	☐
3	What was Tarzan's title as a nobleman?	☐
4	Finish the world's first phone conversation: 'Mr. Watson come here … '	☐
5	What colors are 'The Wiggles' shirts?	☐

☑ for correct answer, ☒ for wrong answer.

SCORE:

Answers: 1) Dr. Seuss 2) They put them on their feet 3) The Earl of Greystoke 4) I want to see you 5) Red, yellow, blue & purple

Game Five - Total

Who will be inducted into the Family Hall of Fame or Shame?
Add up all the rounds and let's find out who the winner is!

Kids	Parents
Round One (+ bonus points):	Round One (+ bonus points):
Round Two (+ bonus points):	Round Two (+ bonus points):
Bonus round:	Bonus round:
Total:	Total:

Write your names where they belong. Will it be the Family Hall of Fame,
or the embarrassing Family Hall of Shame? See pages 174 and 175.

game six

How are you doing so far?
There are another three rounds for each
team coming up, so make them count.

Kids - Round One

Parents, get ready to ask the kids these questions. Each correct answer is worth 1 point. If you get them all right, score a bonus 2 points!

1	What is a Russian astronaut called?	☐
2	What is a Hawaiian flower necklace?	☐
3	Is 'Pink Floyd' a cocktail or a rock band?	☐
4	What date is Valentine's Day?	☐
5	In which country were the first Olympic Games held?	☐

☑ for correct answer, ☒ for wrong answer.

SCORE:

Answers: 1) Cosmonaut 2) A lei 3) A rock band 4) February 14th 5) Greece

Parents - Round One

Kids, ask the parents these five questions. Every correct answer scores 1 point. Get all five right and score a bonus 2 points.

1	Where is Fangorn Forest?	☐
2	In the 'Lion King', who is the evil, greedy lion?	☐
3	Sonic the Hedgehog is a mascot for what gaming system?	☐
4	What is the most popular sport in South America?	☐
5	While a vampire bat is sipping blood, what else is it doing?	☐

☑ for correct answer, ☒ for wrong answer.

SCORE:

Kids - Round Two

Parents, ask the kids these five questions. Every correct answer is worth 1 point. Get them all correct and score 2 bonus points.

1	What is a tooth doctor called?	☐
2	What country won the World Cup in 2006?	☐
3	What device did Apple introduce in 2001?	☐
4	What is a kiln?	☐
5	Do peas grow on a tree, a bush or a vine?	☐

☑ for correct answer, ☒ for wrong answer.

SCORE:

Answers: 1) Dentist 2) Italy 3) The iPod 4) An oven 5) A vine

Parents - Round Two

Kids, it's your turn to ask the parents their five questions. Every correct answer is worth 1 point. Get all five right and score a bonus 2 points.

1	True or False? Caterpillars have five times as many muscles as humans.	☐
2	What is the name of the amusement park devoted to Lego?	☐
3	In 'Harry Potter', what does Hermione use to go back in time?	☐
4	What is a pirate's sword called?	☐
5	Who built the world's first theaters: the Egyptians, Greeks or Romans?	☐

☑ for correct answer, ☒ for wrong answer.

SCORE:

Answers: 1) False – they have three times as many 2) Legoland 3) Time Turner 4) A cutlass 5) Greeks

Kids - Bonus Round

Okay, kids, it's bonus time. Each correct answer is worth 3 points. Parents, ask away.

1	What color do you get if you mix yellow and blue?	☐
2	What are 'jodhpurs'?	☐
3	What country does 'karaoke' come from?	☐
4	Who wrote 'Tom Sawyer'?	☐
5	What is 'calligraphy'?	☐

☑ for correct answer, ☒ for wrong answer.

SCORE:

Parents - Bonus Round

Parents, it's your chance to earn some bonus points. Each correct answer is worth 3 points. Kids, it's your turn to do the asking.

1	What color is Barney the Dinosaur's friend BJ?	☐
2	What does a flying 'Vortex' look like?	☐
3	In Karate, what color belt comes after blue?	☐
4	In Disney's 'Beauty and the Beast', what does Belle's father do for a living?	☐
5	What was the first living thing to travel in space?	☐
		SCORE:

☑ for correct answer, ☒ for wrong answer.

Game Six - Total

Who will be inducted into the Family Hall of Fame or Shame?
Add up all the rounds and let's find out who the winner is!

Kids	Parents
Round One (+ bonus points):	Round One (+ bonus points):
Round Two (+ bonus points):	Round Two (+ bonus points):
Bonus round:	Bonus round:
Total:	Total:

Write your names where they belong. Will it be the Family Hall of Fame,
or the embarrassing Family Hall of Shame? See pages 174 and 175.

game seven

The Family Halls of Fame or Shame await you after every game. Let's make it the Hall of Fame for game seven.

Kids - Round One

Parents, it's time to see how much the kids know about the older generation. A correct answer scores 1 point, with a bonus 2 points if all answers are correct. Ask away!

1	What color are robins' eggs?	☐
2	In 'The Addams Family' what is 'Thing'?	☐
3	What is a baby kangaroo called?	☐
4	Who is Donald Duck's girlfriend?	☐
5	If you are near-sighted, what can't you see?	☐

☑ for correct answer, ☒ for wrong answer.

SCORE:

Answers: 1) Blue 2) A hand 3) A joey 4) Daisy Duck 5) Things far away

Parents - Round One

Okay, kids, it's your turn to quiz the parents. Let's see how they go with the first five questions. Take it away!

1	Which company makes Bionicle™ toys?	☐
2	Which ancient people worshipped the beetle?	☐
3	The possum is considered what kind of animal?	☐
4	How many characters did Eddie Murphy play in 'The Nutty Professor'?	☐
5	What food is used to make dynamite: rice, peanuts or apples?	☐

SCORE:

☑ for correct answer, ☒ for wrong answer.

Kids - Round Two

Here's another chance for the kids to score up to 7 points (if they get all the answers right!). Parents, take it away.

1	What cheese has holes in it?	☐
2	Which country did the Pilgrims come from?	☐
3	You eat one quarter of a candy bar. How much is left?	☐
4	What is a 'sombrero'?	☐
5	What is special about a chameleon?	☐

☑ for correct answer, ☒ for wrong answer.

SCORE:

Parents - Round Two

Okay, kids, let's see how the parents go with the next five questions. Keep score and remember to add 2 bonus points if they deserve them!

1	Who wrote 'The Tortoise and The Hare'?	☐
2	In 'The Lord of the Rings', who is Brego?	☐
3	What is the sweatiest part of your body?	☐
4	What are the names of the two agents in 'Men in Black'?	☐
5	What size is the Grinch's heart?	☐

SCORE:

☑ for correct answer, ☒ for wrong answer.

Kids - Bonus Round

It's bonus time for the kids. Five questions worth 3 points each.
Parents, ask away!

1	Which car company made the 'Silver Ghost'?	☐
2	What is the proper name for a 'twister'?	☐
3	What two parts of your body do you breathe air through?	☐
4	What are the leather shoes worn by Native Americans called?	☐
5	What is the center of an apple called?	☐

☑ for correct answer, ☒ for wrong answer.

SCORE:

Answers: 1) Rolls Royce 2) Tornado 3) Nose and mouth 4) Moccasins 5) Core

Parents - Bonus Round

Okay, Kids, it's time for the parents to see how many bonus points they can pick up. The pressure's on - start asking!

1	Who wrote 'Dracula'?	☐
2	How do mother crocodiles carry their babies?	☐
3	In 'Dungeons and Dragons', who is the main storyteller?	☐
4	What city does Stuart Little live in?	☐
5	What is the most popular take-out food in the USA?	☐

SCORE:

☑ for correct answer, ☒ for wrong answer.

1) Bram Stoker 2) In their open mouths 3) The Dungeon Master 4) New York 5) Pizza

Game Seven - Total

Who will be inducted into the Family Hall of Fame or Shame?
Add up all the rounds and let's find out who the winner is!

Kids
Round One (+ bonus points):
Round Two (+ bonus points):
Bonus round:
Total:

Parents
Round One (+ bonus points):
Round Two (+ bonus points):
Bonus round:
Total:

Write your names where they belong. Will it be the Family Hall of Fame,
or the embarrassing Family Hall of Shame? See pages 174 and 175.

game eight

can the parents outdo the kids in game eight? And don't forget - those bonus points could make or break you!

Kids - Round One

Okay, parents, let's see how well the kids do with the first five questions. 1 point for each correct answer and 2 bonus points for a perfect round.

1	When it rains hard, what animals is it said to rain?	☐
2	'Bollywood' refers to the huge movie industry in what country?	☐
3	What are Ray-Bans™?	☐
4	Who is the famous singer father of Enrique Iglesias?	☐
5	In which city is the Louvre?	☐

☑ for correct answer, ☒ for wrong answer.

SCORE:

Parents - Round One

Another game and another five questions for the parents. Be sure to add their 2 bonus points if they manage to get five correct answers.

1	What is Dr. Jekyll's first name?	☐
2	Who was the first US President to appear on TV?	☐
3	What cartoon did Mickey Mouse first appear in?	☐
4	What kind of creature is a 'flying dragon'?	☐
5	What do the seven spikes on the crown of the Statue of Liberty stand for?	☐

☑ for correct answer, ☒ for wrong answer.

SCORE:

Answers: 1) Henry 2) Franklin D. Roosevelt 3) Steamboat Willie 4) A lizard 5) The seven continents and the seven seas

Kids - Round Two

Five more questions for the kids. Let's see how well they do this round. Parents, ask away.

1	Is a 'rhododendron' a flower, insect or hat?	☐
2	Who first voiced Mickey Mouse?	☐
3	What do Pandas eat?	☐
4	Who wrote 'Romeo and Juliet'?	☐
5	What do you do with mulch?	☐

☑ for correct answer, ☒ for wrong answer.

SCORE:

Parents - Round Two

Another five questions for the kids to ask the parents. Let's find out just how smart they are.

1	Which TV show started a dance craze called the 'Batusi'?	☐
2	In which Italian region is the city of Pisa?	☐
3	How long is a 'jiffy'?	☐
4	Who is the middle sibling on 'The Simpsons'?	☐
5	What does a puffer fish do in order to blow up into a ball?	☐

☑ for correct answer, ☒ for wrong answer.

SCORE:

Answers: 1) Batman 2) Tuscany 3) 1/100th of a second 4) Lisa 5) Swallow water

Kids - Bonus Round

This is the last chance for the Kids to increase their score. Luckily, each correct answer is worth 3 points. Parents, start asking!

1	You and your three friends each have two CDs. How many do you have altogether?	☐
2	Is a 'Phillips head' a hammer, screwdriver or nail?	☐
3	What country invented pizza?	☐
4	How often are the Winter Olympics held?	☐
5	Which note follows 're' on the musical scale?	☐

☑ for correct answer, ☒ for wrong answer.

SCORE:

Answers: 1) Eight 2) A screwdriver 3) Italy 4) Every four years 5) Mi

Parents - Bonus Round

Kids, it's your turn to quiz the parents in the Bonus round.
Let's see how smart they are.

1	True or False? Karate originated in Korea.	☐
2	What kind of creature is Pikachu?	☐
3	What is the name of Sabrina's talking black cat?	☐
4	What is an earthquake on the moon called?	☐
5	What do bombardier beetles do in order to fend off their enemies?	☐

☑ for correct answer, ☒ for wrong answer.

SCORE:

Answers: 1) False – in India 2) An electric mouse 3) Salem 4) A moonquake 5) They pass wind!

Game Eight - Total

Who will be inducted into the Family Hall of Fame or Shame?
Add up all the rounds and let's find out who the winner is!

Kids
Round One (+ bonus points):
Round Two (+ bonus points):
Bonus round:
Total:

Parents
Round One (+ bonus points):
Round Two (+ bonus points):
Bonus round:
Total:

Write your names where they belong. Will it be the Family Hall of Fame, or the embarrassing Family Hall of Shame? See pages 174 and 175.

game nine

who said that parents know everything?
come on, kids - this next game could be
your best game yet!

Kids - Round One

Parents, it's another game and another five questions for the kids.
Let's find out how smart they are.

1	What are the three primary colors?	☐
2	What is the name given to any pirate's flag?	☐
3	What is an Alaskan snow dog?	☐
4	What two colors are zebras?	☐
5	What do you want if you send an S.O.S. signal?	☐

☑ for correct answer, ☒ for wrong answer.

SCORE:

Answers: 1) Red, blue and yellow 2) The Jolly Roger 3) A husky 4) Black and white 5) Help

Parents - Round One

Kids, here's the first five questions for the parents. 1 point for each correct answer and 2 bonus points if they get them all right.

1	What was Harry Potter's Daniel Radcliffe doing when he was discovered?	☐
2	What was the first toy advertised on TV?	☐
3	What languages do the Ents speak?	☐
4	True or False? In 'The Love Bug', Herbie's number is 69.	☐
5	What language does cartoon character 'Dora the Explorer' teach kids?	☐

☑ for correct answer, ☒ for wrong answer.

SCORE:

Answers: 1) Watching a play 2) Mr. Potato Head 3) Entish and Old Entish 4) False – it's 53 5) Spanish

Kids - Round Two

Take it away, parents, with the next five questions for the kids. 1 point for every correct answer and 2 bonus points for a perfect round.

1	In which city is the Colosseum?	☐
2	What do you do with 'Baked Alaska'?	☐
3	What is 'rhinoplasty'?	☐
4	How many people ride on a tandem bicycle?	☐
5	What city starting with 'V' does the Pope live in?	☐

☑ for correct answer, ☒ for wrong answer.

SCORE:

Answers: 1) Rome 2) Eat it - it's a dessert 3) A nose job 4) Two or more 5) Vatican City

Parents - Round Two

Kids, let's take it away with another five questions for the parents.
There's 7 points up for grabs, so start asking!

1	Which snake can kill an elephant?	☐
2	Who devised the first wet suit for divers?	☐
3	Kryptonite is an actual substance. True or false ?	☐
4	What country made the first donuts?	☐
5	When you mix wormwood with asphodel, what do you get?	☐

SCORE:

☑ for correct answer, ☒ for wrong answer.

Kids - Bonus Round

Okay, parents, here's five bonus questions for the kids.
They'll score 3 points for every correct answer.

1	Finish this: 'If it ain't broke....'	☐
2	Which city is called 'The Big Apple'?	☐
3	True or False? A person from Greenland is a 'Greenie'.	☐
4	What were Pavarotti, Domingo and Carreras known as?	☐
5	What is 'gin rummy'?	☐

☑ for correct answer, ☒ for wrong answer.

SCORE:

Parents - Bonus Round

Only five questions to go and the last chance for the parents to improve their score. Take it away, Kids!

1	What would you do with a 'drupe'?	☐
2	How old was Bill Gates when he launched his business career?	☐
3	What are the world's noisiest monkeys?	☐
4	Who invented the scissors?	☐
5	Which US state has the longest coastline?	☐

☑ for correct answer, ☒ for wrong answer.

SCORE:

Game Nine - Total

Who will be inducted into the Family Hall of Fame or Shame?
Add up all the rounds and let's find out who the winner is!

Kids
Round One (+ bonus points):
Round Two (+ bonus points):
Bonus round:
Total:

Parents
Round One (+ bonus points):
Round Two (+ bonus points):
Bonus round:
Total:

Write your names where they belong. Will it be the Family Hall of Fame,
or the embarrassing Family Hall of Shame? See pages 174 and 175.

game ten

Well done. You've made it to game ten and the halfway mark. Is your team proving its superiority, or are you wallowing in mediocrity?

Kids - Round One

Here we go again with five questions for the kids. A maximum of 7 points is up for grabs if the kids manage a perfect round, so ask away, parents.

1	Which word is the pronoun? 'She spoke on the cell phone.'	☐
2	What food does the flying fox like best?	☐
3	What kind of peppers did Peter Piper pick?	☐
4	What vehicle takes you to hospital in an emergency?	☐
5	What creates hydro-electricity?	☐

☑ for correct answer, ☒ for wrong answer.

SCORE:

Answers: 1) She 2) Fruit 3) Pickled peppers 4) An ambulance 5) Water

Parents - Round One

Kids, here's five questions for the parents. Let's see how smart they are.

1	Which type of camel has only one hump?	☐
2	What is the world's largest Tyrannosaurus Rex called?	☐
3	What is the world's heaviest beetle?	☐
4	Who wrote 'Twinkle Twinkle Little Star'?	☐
5	Robert Van Winkle is the real name of which one-hit-wonder rapper?	☐

☑ for correct answer, ☒ for wrong answer.

SCORE:

Answers: 1) The dromedary 2) Sue 3) The Goliath beetle 4) Mozart 5) Vanilla Ice

Kids - Round Two

Parents, it's your turn to ask the kids another five questions.
Let's see how they go this round. Take it away!

1	Is your hair dead or alive?	☐
2	What are the vast, dry areas on the moon called?	☐
3	What is a 'Chinese junk'?	☐
4	In the future, what will the present be?	☐
5	What is a rabbit's underground home called?	☐

☑ for correct answer, ☒ for wrong answer.

SCORE:

Answers: 1) Dead 2) Seas 3) A boat 4) The past 5) Warren

Parents - Round Two

Five questions down and here's another five for the kids to ask the parents. Let's see how they go in this round.

1	What is SpongeBob's surname?	☐
2	In bowling, what do you call three strikes in a row?	☐
3	What do 'Foo Fighters' do?	☐
4	What is Gollum's real name?	☐
5	In what sport do you find a 'stalefish'?	☐

SCORE:

☑ for correct answer, ☒ for wrong answer.

Kids - Bonus Round

It's make or break time with these five bonus questions for the kids.
Parents, take it away!

1	What is the outer layer of the earth called?	☐
2	Name Mick Jagger's famous band.	☐
3	What do you call the imaginary line that divides countries or states?	☐
4	What is a group of lions?	☐
5	What is London's 'Big Ben'?	☐

☑ for correct answer, ☒ for wrong answer.

SCORE:

Parents - Bonus Round

Kids, here's five bonus questions to ask the parents. Each correct answer is worth 3 points. Let's see how they go!

1	Which country has the most islands?	☐
2	How old is Elmo?	☐
3	What is the first name of Indiana Jones?	☐
4	Which studio made 'Toy Story'?	☐
5	What is the capital of Australia?	☐

☑ for correct answer, ☒ for wrong answer.

SCORE:

Game Ten - Total

Who will be inducted into the Family Hall of Fame or Shame?
Add up all the rounds and let's find out who the winner is!

Kids	Parents
Round One (+ bonus points):	Round One (+ bonus points):
Round Two (+ bonus points):	Round Two (+ bonus points):
Bonus round:	Bonus round:
Total:	Total:

Write your names where they belong. Will it be the Family Hall of Fame,
or the embarrassing Family Hall of Shame? See pages 174 and 175.

game eleven

Here comes game eleven. Parents read
the first set of questions and then it's up to
the kids to beat the parents. Good luck.

Kids - Round One

Parents, get ready to ask the kids these questions. Each correct answer is worth 1 point. If you get them all right, score a bonus 2 points!

1	Which one is a 'feline': cat, flea or seal?	☐
2	What is 'Bilbo'?	☐
3	What kind of movies did Alfred Hitchcock make?	☐
4	What are blue jeans made of?	☐
5	What is the name of Mickey Mouse's girlfriend?	☐

☑ for correct answer, ☒ for wrong answer.

SCORE:

Answers: 1) Cat 2) A Hobbit 3) Thrillers 4) Denim 5) Minnie Mouse

Parents - Round One

Kids, ask the parents these five questions. Every correct answer scores 1 point. Get all five right and score a bonus 2 points.

1	Who wrote 'The Time Machine'?	☐
2	What two things are in a Polaroid i-Zone camera?	☐
3	Which Xbox game features a cat whose job it is to manufacture time?	☐
4	What does an alligator do to warn off its enemies?	☐
5	What color is Mr. Spock's blood?	☐

☑ for correct answer, ☒ for wrong answer.

SCORE:

Answers: 1) H.G. Wells 2) Camera & FM radio 3) Blinx: The Time Sweeper 4) It hisses 5) Green

Kids - Round Two

Parents, ask the kids these five questions. Every correct answer is worth 1 point. Get them all correct and score 2 bonus points.

1	How long can a polar bear stay under water?	☐
2	What does an anti-oxidant do?	☐
3	What country is the Taj Mahal in?	☐
4	Is a 'fedora' a tool, a tree or a hat?	☐
5	Where are the IKEA headquarters located?	☐

☑ for correct answer, ☒ for wrong answer.

SCORE:

Answers: 1) Two minutes 2) It improves your immune system and helps keep you healthy 3) India 4) A hat 5) Sweden

Parents - Round Two

Kids, it's your turn to ask the parents their five questions. Every correct answer is worth 1 point. Get all five right and score a bonus 2 points.

1	In 'Peanuts', who carries around a blanket?	☐
2	Whose friends are Toby, Rusty, Annie and James?	☐
3	If you were doing 'double barspins', what would you be doing?	☐
4	What are the largest worker ants called?	☐
5	In a ballet studio, dancers hold onto a barre. Spell 'barre.'	☐

☑ for correct answer, ☒ for wrong answer.

SCORE:

Answers: 1) Linus 2) Thomas the Tank Engine 3) BMX bike riding 4) Soldiers 5) B.A.R.R.E.

91

Kids - Bonus Round

Okay, kids, it's bonus time. Each correct answer is worth 3 points.
Parents, ask away.

1	Which one would you NOT put in a cake: flour, butter, wasabi or eggs?	☐
2	What is a group of crows called?	☐
3	Who is 'the boy who never grows up'?	☐
4	Which elephant has the largest ears: African or Asian?	☐
5	What is a 'Lazy Susan'?	☐

☑ for correct answer, ☒ for wrong answer.

SCORE:

Answers: 1) Wasabi 2) A murder 3) Peter Pan 4) African 5) A turntable

Parents - Bonus Round

Parents, it's your chance to earn some bonus points. Each correct answer is worth 3 points. Kids, it's your turn to do the asking.

1	What is Inspector Gadget's job?	☐
2	Name the seven dwarfs in 'Snow White'.	☐
3	What is the name of the monkey in 'Dora the Explorer'?	☐
4	Relative to its size and weight, which creature is the best jumper?	☐
5	What was Thomas Edison's middle name?	☐

SCORE:

☑ for correct answer, ☒ for wrong answer.

Game Eleven - Total

Who will be inducted into the Family Hall of Fame or Shame?
Add up all the rounds and let's find out who the winner is!

Kids
Round One (+ bonus points):
Round Two (+ bonus points):
Bonus round:
Total:

Parents
Round One (+ bonus points):
Round Two (+ bonus points):
Bonus round:
Total:

Write your names where they belong. Will it be the Family Hall of Fame,
or the embarrassing Family Hall of Shame? See pages 174 and 175.

game twelve

Remember, you're not just playing for yourself,
you're representing your entire generation!
Are you ready for game twelve?

Kids - Round One

Parents, it's time to see how much the kids know about the older generation. A correct answer scores 1 point, with a bonus 2 points if all answers are correct. Ask away!

1	What are 'mung beans': beans, stones or sprouts?	☐
2	What must you put on your head when you go bike riding?	☐
3	How many sides does an octagon have?	☐
4	What is a 'pogo stick'?	☐
5	On an Internet address, what does 'www' stand for?	☐

☑ for correct answer, ☒ for wrong answer.

SCORE:

Answers: 1) Sprouts 2) A helmet 3) Eight 4) A jumping toy 5) World wide web

Parents - Round One

Okay, kids, it's your turn to quiz the parents. Let's see how they go with the first five questions. Take it away!

1	What bird can hover like a helicopter?	☐
2	What was the name of the rat who became a chef in Disney's 'Ratatouille'?	☐
3	Dung Beetles eat horn flies and what else?	☐
4	What are 'the 3 steps to eating an Oreo'?	☐
5	In 'Where's Waldo?', what color shirt does Waldo wear?	☐

☑ for correct answer, ☒ for wrong answer.

SCORE:

Answers: 1) Hummingbird 2) Remy 3) Poop 4) Twist, lick and dunk 5) Red and white striped

Kids - Round Two

Here's another chance for the kids to score up to 7 points (if they get all the answers right!). Parents, take it away.

1	What do you use a thimble for?	☐
2	Which is a music award: a Grammy, an Emmy or a Britney?	☐
3	What country does tartan come from?	☐
4	What kind of animal is 'Lassie'?	☐
5	How long does it take for the sand to flow through an egg timer?	☐

☑ for correct answer, ☒ for wrong answer.

SCORE:

Parents - Round Two

Okay, kids, let's see how the parents go with the next five questions. Keep score and remember to add 2 bonus points if they deserve them!

1	What country does Orlando Bloom come from?	☐
2	What popular kids product does Sanrio create?	☐
3	Which Shakespearan play features the character of Yorick?	☐
4	Who played Willy Wonka in Tim Burton's movie remake?	☐
5	What is Jack Sparrow's profession?	☐

☑ for correct answer, ☒ for wrong answer.

SCORE:

Answers: 1) England 2) Hello Kitty 3) Hamlet 4) Johnny Depp 5) Pirate

Kids - Bonus Round

It's bonus time for the kids. Five questions worth 3 points each.
Parents, ask away!

1	What is a P.I.?	☐
2	What animal brings Easter eggs?	☐
3	Ships and planes mysteriously disappear in the Bermuda what: square, circle or triangle?	☐
4	Who wrote 'The Jungle Book'?	☐
5	What do you call a scary dream?	☐

SCORE:

☑ for correct answer, ☒ for wrong answer.

Answers: 1) A Private Investigator 2) The Easter Bunny 3) Triangle 4) Rudyard Kipling 5) A nightmare

Parents - Bonus Round

Okay, kids, it's time for the parents to see how many bonus points they can pick up. The pressure's on - start asking!

1	What gaming system did Nintendo release in 2007?	☐
2	In 'Star Wars, Episode 1', what is the name of the young queen of Naboo?	☐
3	Where does the Mario Brothers video game take place?	☐
4	Name Hannah Montana's schoolgirl alter-ego?	☐
5	What is the female character's name in 'Beauty and the Beast'?	☐

☑ for correct answer, ☒ for wrong answer.

SCORE:

Answers: 1) The Wii 2) Queen Amidala 3) The Mushroom Kingdom 4) Miley Stewart 5) Belle

Game Twelve - Total

Who will be inducted into the Family Hall of Fame or Shame?
Add up all the rounds and let's find out who the winner is!

Kids	Parents
Round One (+ bonus points):	Round One (+ bonus points):
Round Two (+ bonus points):	Round Two (+ bonus points):
Bonus round:	Bonus round:
Total:	Total:

Write your names where they belong. Will it be the Family Hall of Fame,
or the embarrassing Family Hall of Shame? See pages 174 and 175.

game thirteen

Game thirteen - unlucky for some,
but maybe this is your chance to score
some points and prove who's boss!
Good luck and let the game begin!

Kids - Round One

Okay, parents, let's see how well the kids do with the first five questions. 1 point for each correct answer and 2 bonus points for a perfect round.

1	What type of animal chews and regurgitates 'cud'?	☐
2	Which continent is located at the South Pole?	☐
3	Which sees better: an eagle or a lion?	☐
4	What star sign is represented by a lion: Taurus, Capricorn or Leo?	☐
5	What is a 'cubicle'?	☐

☑ for correct answer, ☒ for wrong answer.

SCORE:

Answers: 1) Cows 2) Antarctica 3) Eagle 4) Leo 5) A partially enclosed workspace

Parents - Round One

Another game and another five questions for the parents. Be sure to add their 2 bonus points if they manage to get five correct answers.

1	What is the largest country, in terms of area?	☐
2	What do you call the smallest animal in a litter?	☐
3	In the game 'Ro-Sham-Bo', what beats scissors?	☐
4	Name the Wright Brothers' first airplane.	☐
5	Are sharks considered fish, marsupials, or mammals?	☐

SCORE:

☑ for correct answer, ☒ for wrong answer.

Kids - Round Two

Five more questions for the kids. Let's see how well they do this round. Parents, ask away.

1	Who painted the 'Sistine Chapel': Michelangelo or Picasso?	☐
2	Sing the next line: 'Row, row, row your boat …'	☐
3	What is 'claustrophobia' a fear of?	☐
4	What does the 'rook' piece resemble, in the game of chess?	☐
5	Which are more kids allergic to: candy, cow's milk or school?	☐

☑ for correct answer, ☒ for wrong answer.

SCORE:

Answers: 1) Michelangelo 2) Gently down the stream 3) Closed or small spaces 4) Castle 5) Cow's milk

Parents - Round Two

Another five questions for the kids to ask the parents. Let's find out just how smart they are.

1	What is the gymnastics term for the type of cartwheel where both feet land at the same time?	☐
2	From which country did spaghetti originate?	☐
3	What is the second longest river in the world?	☐
4	Would you weigh more or less if you were on Mars?	☐
5	Which stylish dolls are made for girls with a 'passion for fashion'?	☐

☑ for correct answer, ☒ for wrong answer.

SCORE:

Answers: 1) A round-off 2) China 3) Amazon 4) Less 5) Bratz

Kids - Bonus Round

This is the last chance for the kids to increase their score. Luckily, each correct answer is worth 3 points. Parents, start asking!

1	Where does a beaver live?	☐
2	Which way do crabs walk?	☐
3	How long does it take for the Earth to travel around the Sun?	☐
4	In what country would you find The Sphinx?	☐
5	True or False? All camels have 2 humps.	☐

☑ for correct answer, ☒ for wrong answer.

SCORE:

Answers: 1) In a lodge 2) Sideways 3) One year 4) Egypt 5) False

Parents - Bonus Round

Kids, it's your turn to quiz the parents in the Bonus round. Let's see how smart they are.

1	What is the name of the planet where Luke Skywalker is from?	☐
2	What is the world's largest lake?	☐
3	What are baby alligators called?	☐
4	What is a group of butterflies called?	☐
5	What do you call a scientist who studies dinosaurs?	☐

SCORE:

☑ for correct answer, ☒ for wrong answer.

Answers: 1) Tatooine 2) The Caspian Sea 3) Hatchlings 4) A flutter 5) A paleontologist

Game Thirteen - Total

Who will be inducted into the Family Hall of Fame or Shame?
Add up all the rounds and let's find out who the winner is!

Kids	Parents
Round One (+ bonus points):	Round One (+ bonus points):
Round Two (+ bonus points):	Round Two (+ bonus points):
Bonus round:	Bonus round:
Total:	Total:

Write your names where they belong. Will it be the Family Hall of Fame,
or the embarrassing Family Hall of Shame? See pages 174 and 175.

game fourteen

can the kids really beat the parents?
or will the parents outwit the kids?
Put your brains in gear and let's find out!

Kids - Round One

Parents, it's another game and another five questions for the kids. Let's find out how smart they are.

1	What is 'sashimi'?	☐
2	Which team sport is played on a diamond?	☐
3	What is the proper name for your belly button?	☐
4	What does "QWERTY" refer to?	☐
5	Is a piranha a basket, a fish or a boat?	☐

☑ for correct answer, ☒ for wrong answer.

SCORE:

Answers: 1) Raw fish - yum! 2) Baseball 3) Navel 4) A modern keyboard 5) Fish

Parents - Round One

Kids, here's the first five questions for the parents. 1 point for each correct answer and 2 bonus points if they get them all right.

1	What is singer Beyonce's last name?	☐
2	Who is the protagonist in 'Catcher in the Rye'?	☐
3	In what continent is the language Hausa spoken?	☐
4	Which birds are flightless: penguins, ostriches, or emus?	☐
5	What does it mean to "comment" someone on Myspace?	☐

☑ for correct answer, ☒ for wrong answer.

SCORE:

Answers: 1) Knowles 2) Holden Caulfield 3) Africa 4) All of them 5) Leave a message in their comment box

Kids - Round Two

Take it away, parents, with the next five questions for the kids. 1 point for every correct answer and 2 bonus points for a perfect round.

1	What is the capital of Canada?	☐
2	What is a 'pistachio': a pistol, a nut or a beetle?	☐
3	How do people in France say 'thank you'?	☐
4	Where would you find Tweedledum and Tweedledee?	☐
5	What are French fries made from?	☐

☑ for correct answer, ☒ for wrong answer.

SCORE:

Answers: 1) Ottawa 2) A nut 3) Merci 4) In Wonderland 5) Potatoes

Parents - Round Two

Kids, let's take it away with another five questions for the parents.
There's 7 points up for grabs, so start asking!

1	What is the name of the world's biggest passenger plane, introduced in 2007?	☐
2	Which skateboarder invented the 'Fingerflip Backside Air', and 'Ollie 540'?	☐
3	What is Linus' last name in the 'Peanuts' comic strip?	☐
4	Which actor was Brad Pitt's first wife?	☐
5	What is a 'yeti'?	☐

☑ for correct answer, ☒ for wrong answer.

SCORE:

Kids - Bonus Round

Okay, parents, here's five bonus questions for the kids.
They'll score 3 points for every correct answer.

1	When Mozart wrote his first opera, was he 12, 20 or 22 years old?	☐
2	What does a dragon breathe out?	☐
3	In the old days, why did women wear a 'bustle'?	☐
4	What is a tomato: a vegetable, fruit or herb?	☐
5	What is the capital of Finland?	☐

☑ for correct answer, ☒ for wrong answer.

SCORE:

Answers: 1) 12 2) Fire 3) To make their butts look bigger 4) Fruit 5) Helsinki!

Parents - Bonus Round

Only five questions to go and the last chance for the parents to improve their score. Take it away, kids!

1	Which is not a Spice Girl: Posh, Wasabi, Ginger or Scary?	☐
2	What is the name of the American sports team that David Beckham joined in 2007?	☐
3	What is the second highest mountain in the world?	☐
4	What did Howard Carter discover in 1922?	☐
5	What is the strongest, heaviest and longest bone in the human body?	☐

☑ for correct answer, ☒ for wrong answer.

SCORE:

Game Fourteen - Total

Who will be inducted into the Family Hall of Fame or Shame?
Add up all the rounds and let's find out who the winner is!

Kids	Parents
Round One (+ bonus points):	Round One (+ bonus points):
Round Two (+ bonus points):	Round Two (+ bonus points):
Bonus round:	Bonus round:
Total:	Total:

Write your names where they belong. Will it be the Family Hall of Fame,
or the embarrassing Family Hall of Shame? See pages 174 and 175.

game fifteen

After 14 games, there's no better time
to prove you're up to the challenge.
Let's see who can win game fifteen.

Kids - Round One

Here we go again with five questions for the kids. A maximum of 7 points is up for grabs if the kids manage a perfect round, so ask away, parents.

1	What is water surrounding a castle called?	☐
2	What is a 'ladybird': a beetle, bird or spider?	☐
3	Finish this old saying: 'Let sleeping dogs ... '	☐
4	What large waterfall borders the US and Canada?	☐
5	Name the 2 flavors in 'marble cake'?	☐

☑ for correct answer, ☒ for wrong answer.

SCORE:

Answers: 1) A moat 2) A beetle 3) Lie 4) Niagara Falls 5) Vanilla and chocolate

Parents - Round One

Kids, here's five questions for the parents. Let's see how smart they are.

1	How much does the Park Place property cost in 'Monopoly'?		☐
2	What Stephen King novel is based on a scary clown?		☐
3	Disney's 'High School Musical' is based on what famous tale?		☐
4	What always helps get Dora the Explorer out of a bind?		☐
5	What is the tagline for 'Transformers'?		☐

☑ for correct answer, ☒ for wrong answer.

SCORE:

Answers: 1) 350 2) It 3) Romeo & Juliet 4) Her backpack 5) More than meets the eye

Kids - Round Two

Parents, it's your turn to ask the kids another five questions.
Let's see how they go this round. Take it away!

1	What is another name for an 'Alsatian' dog?	☐
2	What does R.E.M. stand for?	☐
3	What is "PJs" short for?	☐
4	In which American city would you find the Empire State Building?	☐
5	What is 'Obi-Wan-Kanobi': a robot, an android or a human?	☐

☑ for correct answer, ☒ for wrong answer.

SCORE:

Answers: 1) German Shepherd 2) Rapid Eye Movement 3) Pyjamas 4) New York 5) Human

Parents - Round Two

Kids, it's your turn to ask the parents their five questions. Every correct answer is worth 1 point. Get all five right and score a bonus 2 points.

1	What was NOT one of the original songs on Guitar Hero: 'Bark at the Moon', 'Smoke on the Water', or 'Wannabe'?		☐
2	How did the other reindeer treat Rudolph?		☐
3	Who did Mr. Incredible marry?		☐
4	In 'Harry Potter', pickle, earthworm and earwax are flavors of which candy?		☐
5	Who shot Montgomery Burns?		☐

SCORE:

☑ for correct answer, ☒ for wrong answer.

Answers: 1) Wannabe 2) They laughed and called him names 3) Elastigirl 4) Bertie Bott's Every Flavor Beans 5) Maggie Simpson

Kids - Bonus Round

It's make or break time with these five bonus questions for the kids. Parents, take it away!

1	What type of creature is 'Black Beauty'?	☐
2	If you are 'the cat's meow', are you sneaky, wonderful or playful?	☐
3	Who reads 'Braille'?	☐
4	Yes or No: do polar bears live in Antarctica?	☐
5	What is another name for a 'Flower Child'?	☐

☑ for correct answer, ☒ for wrong answer.

SCORE:

Answers: 1) A horse 2) Wonderful 3) Blind people 4) No 5) Hippie

Parents - Bonus Round

Kids, here's five bonus questions to ask the parents. Each correct answer is worth 3 points. Let's see how they go!

1	What 'professional' service does Peanuts' character Lucy provide?	☐
2	What does Pocahontas' name mean?	☐
3	Who wrote the book 'Jurassic Park'?	☐
4	Name the largest active volcano in Europe.	☐
5	If you are performing a 'battement', what are you doing?	☐

SCORE:

☑ for correct answer, ☒ for wrong answer.

Answers: 1) Psychiatric advice 2) Little Mischief 3) Michael Crichton 4) Mount Etna 5) A ballet movement

Game Fifteen - Total

Who will be inducted into the Family Hall of Fame or Shame?
Add up all the rounds and let's find out who the winner is!

Kids	Parents
Round One (+ bonus points):	Round One (+ bonus points):
Round Two (+ bonus points):	Round Two (+ bonus points):
Bonus round:	Bonus round:
Total:	Total:

Write your names where they belong. Will it be the Family Hall of Fame,
or the embarrassing Family Hall of Shame? See pages 174 and 175.

game sixteen

A big effort in game sixteen could make all the difference to your status on the Family Hall of Fame page. Good luck.

Kids - Round One

Parents, get ready to ask the kids these questions. Each correct answer is worth 1 point. If you get them all right, score a bonus 2 points!

1	What is a children's doctor called?	☐
2	What cartoon was 'Barney Rubble' in?	☐
3	What side of your brain controls your left hand?	☐
4	What kind of money is also called 'plastic'?	☐
5	What was 'Moby Dick'?	☐

☑ for correct answer, ☒ for wrong answer.

SCORE:

Answers: 1) Pediatrician 2) The Flintstones 3) Right side 4) Credit cards 5) A whale

Parents - Round One

Kids, ask the parents these five questions. Every correct answer scores 1 point. Get all five right and score a bonus 2 points.

1	How many different sections are there on a hopscotch pattern?	☐
2	True or False? A cockroach can live several months without its head.	☐
3	Name the flap of skin that hangs beneath a turkey's chin.	☐
4	True or False? Koalas can go days without sleeping.	☐
5	Does our blood have more white or red blood cells?	☐

☑ for correct answer, ☒ for wrong answer.

SCORE:

Answers: 1) Eight! 2) False! But it can live over a week 3) Wattle 4) False – they sleep up to 16 hours a day 5) Red

Kids - Round Two

Parents, ask the kids these five questions. Every correct answer is worth 1 point. Get them all correct and score 2 bonus points.

1	What are four babies born at the same time called?	☐
2	What is the name of our galaxy?	☐
3	Over what river does the London Bridge cross?	☐
4	In the song 'The 12 Days of Christmas', how many golden rings are there?	☐
5	Are oranges full of vitamin C, calcium or protein?	☐

☑ for correct answer, ☒ for wrong answer.

SCORE:

Answers: 1) Quadruplets 2) The Milky Way 3) The River Thames 4) Five 5) Vitamin C

Parents - Round Two

Kids, it's your turn to ask the parents their five questions. Every correct answer is worth 1 point. Get all five right and score a bonus 2 points.

1	What is the term used to measure the height of a horse?	☐
2	Newts, salamanders and toads are in what family of animals?	☐
3	What is the pig's name in 'Charlotte's Web'?	☐
4	Name the creatures who accompanies The Cat in the Hat in Dr. Seuss' famous book?	☐
5	Where do Whangdoodles and Hornswogglers live?	☐

☑ for correct answer, ☒ for wrong answer.

SCORE:

Answers: 1) Hands 2) Amphibians 3) Wilbur 4) Thing One and Thing Two 5) In Loompaland

Kids - Bonus Round

Okay, kids, it's bonus time. Each correct answer is worth 3 points. Parents, ask away.

1	What is a female bird called: a chick, hen or birdie?	☐
2	What colors are on the German national flag?	☐
3	Finish this slogan: 'Make love not ...'	☐
4	True or False? A boomerang is used to catch animals.	☐
5	What sport does Tiger Woods play?	☐

☑ for correct answer, ☒ for wrong answer.

SCORE:

Answers: 1) A hen 2) Black, red and gold 3) War 4) True 5) Golf

Parents - Bonus Round

Parents, it's your chance to earn some bonus points. Each correct answer is worth 3 points. Kids, it's your turn to do the asking.

1	How many bones are there in the human body?	☐
2	What astrological sign are you if you were born in early June?	☐
3	In what year was the Euro introduced to the world finance market?	☐
4	What is a 'Tamagotchi': a skateboarding trick or an electronic pet?	☐
5	What is the capital city of the the Philippines?	☐

☑ for correct answer, ☒ for wrong answer.

SCORE:

Answers: 1) 206 2) Gemini 3) 1999 4) Electronic pet 5) Manila

Game Sixteen - Total

Who will be inducted into the Family Hall of Fame or Shame?
Add up all the rounds and let's find out who the winner is!

Kids	Parents
Round One (+ bonus points):	Round One (+ bonus points):
Round Two (+ bonus points):	Round Two (+ bonus points):
Bonus round:	Bonus round:
Total:	Total:

Write your names where they belong. Will it be the Family Hall of Fame,
or the embarrassing Family Hall of Shame? See pages 174 and 175.

game seventeen

can the grown-ups measure up to the kids?
Let's see if game seventeen is their lucky game.

Kids - Round One

Parents, it's time to see how much the Kids Know about the older generation. A correct answer scores 1 point, with a bonus 2 points if all answers are correct. Ask away!

1	How long is an Olympic swimming pool?	☐
2	Where is Italy's famous leaning tower located?	☐
3	What does CD stand for?	☐
4	Which animated film features the song, 'Circle of Life'?	☐
5	In what kind of book do you write down the things you do each day?	☐

☑ for correct answer, ☒ for wrong answer.

SCORE:

Answers: 1) 50 meters 2) Pisa 3) Compact Disc 4) The Lion King 5) A diary

Parents - Round One

Okay, kids, it's your turn to quiz the parents. Let's see how they go with the first five questions. Take it away!

1	Americans use dollars, Japanese use yen, but what do Indians use?	☐
2	What is the name of the cat character in the Shrek movies?	☐
3	What is the name of Oscar the Grouch's pet worm?	☐
4	Who is the Norse God of Thunder?	☐
5	Who does Cindy Vortex refer to as 'Spewtron'?	☐

SCORE:

☑ for correct answer, ☒ for wrong answer.

Answers: 1) Rupees 2) Puss in Boots 3) Slimey 4) Thor 5) Jimmy Neutron

Kids - Round Two

Here's another chance for the kids to score up to 7 points (if they get all the answers right!). Parents, take it away.

1	When it's Spring north of the Equator, what season is it south of the Equator?	☐
2	Is Bruce Springsteen known as The Boss, The Leader or The Captain?	☐
3	True or False? You cannot cry in space.	☐
4	What do male Indian Sikhs wear on their heads?	☐
5	How do you say 'goodbye' in Spanish?	☐

☑ for correct answer, ☒ for wrong answer.

SCORE:

Answers: 1) Fall (or Autumn) 2) The Boss 3) True - no gravity, no tears! 4) Turbans 5) Adios

Parents - Round Two

Okay, kids, let's see how the parents go with the next five questions. Keep score and remember to add 2 bonus points if they deserve them!

1	How many players are on the ground in a game of soccer?	☐
2	Give the real name of "He-who-shall-not-be-named."	☐
3	What is the currency of Vatican City?	☐
4	Where would you find the Great Barrier Reef?	☐
5	What is the color of a giraffe's tongue?	☐

SCORE: ☐

☑ for correct answer, ☒ for wrong answer.

Answers: 1) 22 (11 from each team) 2) Lord Voldemort 3) The Euro 4) Off the coast of Queensland, in Australia 5) Black

139

Kids - Bonus Round

It's bonus time for the kids. Five questions worth 3 points each.
Parents, ask away!

1	What are you doing if you are 'tickling the ivories'?	☐
2	What would you do with 'minestrone': eat it or put it in with the dirty clothes?	☐
3	How do you say 'hello' in Spanish?	☐
4	What is a seahorse: a fish, a horse or a reptile?	☐
5	What is a computer screen you touch in order to operate called?	☐

☑ for correct answer, ☒ for wrong answer.

SCORE:

Parents - Bonus Round

Okay, kids, it's time for the parents to see how many bonus points they can pick up. The pressure's on - start asking!

1	What is the name of the outer layer of calcified substance that protects your teeth?	☐
2	True or False? Worms can grow new tails.	☐
3	Name the game starring Peach, Baby Mario and Wario.	☐
4	America Ferrera starred in 'The Sisterhood of the Traveling' what?	☐
5	What river runs through Rome?	SCORE: ☐

☑ for correct answer, ☒ for wrong answer.

Answers: 1) Enamel 2) True 3) Mario Kart 4) Pants 5) The Tiber

Game Seventeen - Total

Who will be inducted into the Family Hall of Fame or Shame?
Add up all the rounds and let's find out who the winner is!

Kids
Round One (+ bonus points):
Round Two (+ bonus points):
Bonus round:
Total:

Parents
Round One (+ bonus points):
Round Two (+ bonus points):
Bonus round:
Total:

Write your names where they belong. Will it be the Family Hall of Fame,
or the embarrassing Family Hall of Shame? See pages 174 and 175.

game eighteen

Show who's really boss in the family,
by making game eighteen your best yet.
Good luck.

Kids - Round One

Okay, parents, let's see how well the kids do with the first five questions. 1 point for each correct answer and 2 bonus points for a perfect round.

1	How many 'c's' are in the word cappuccino?	☐
2	In what sport do you 'dribble'?	☐
3	What building did 'King Kong' climb?	☐
4	What is the head of the Mafia called?	☐
5	What was Noah's boat called?	☐

☑ for correct answer, ☒ for wrong answer.

SCORE:

Parents - Round One

Another game and another five questions for the parents. Be sure to add their 2 bonus points if they manage to get five correct answers.

1	What toy is exactly five-eighths of an inch in diameter?	☐
2	What was the name of Tarzan's chimpanzee?	☐
3	What are you doing if you are 'spelunking'?	☐
4	What did the Chinese invent 2800 years ago, using silk & bamboo?	☐
5	What was the name of Bambi's rabbit friend?	☐

SCORE:

☑ for correct answer, ☒ for wrong answer.

Answers: 1) A basic marble 2) Cheetah 3) You are exploring caves 4) Kites 5) Thumper

145

Kids - Round Two

Five more questions for the kids. Let's see how well they do this round. Parents, ask away.

1	What is a 'hematoma'?	☐
2	Finish this: 'Batman and … '	☐
3	What eating utensils are believed to be invented by the Chinese?	☐
4	A Venus flytrap eats insects. What is it?	☐
5	What animal do we get ham from?	☐

☑ for correct answer, ☒ for wrong answer.

SCORE:

Answers: 1) A bruise 2) Robin 3) Chopsticks 4) A plant 5) Pig

Parents - Round Two

Another five questions for the kids to ask the parents.
Let's find out just how smart they are.

1	What is the heaviest flying insect?	☐
2	What causes 'scurvy'?	☐
3	What is the only contintent bees cannot be found on?	☐
4	Who is Curious George's best friend?	☐
5	What color is Po, the smallest Teletubby?	☐

SCORE:

☑ for correct answer, ☒ for wrong answer.

Kids - Bonus Round

This is the last chance for the kids to increase their score. Luckily, each correct answer is worth 3 points. Parents, start asking!

1	Where do you put mineral salts to soothe your sore muscles?	☐
2	How old do you have to be in most countries to vote?	☐
3	What dogs are white with black spots all over them?	☐
4	Do you sweat to keep warm, cool down or get wet?	☐
5	What is singing without music called?	☐

☑ for correct answer, ☒ for wrong answer.

SCORE:

Answers: 1) In the bath 2) 18 3) Dalmatians 4) Cool down 5) A cappella

Parents - Bonus Round

Kids, it's your turn to quiz the parents in the Bonus round.
Let's see how smart they are.

1	What classical musician from Austria wrote 'The Marriage of Figaro'?	☐
2	What is the capital city of New Zealand?	☐
3	How many sets of wings does the common housefly have?	☐
4	What stadium is named after a ketchup company?	☐
5	What is the name of the nutrient that gives ketchup its famous red color?	☐

☑ for correct answer, ☒ for wrong answer.

SCORE:

Game Eighteen - Total

Who will be inducted into the Family Hall of Fame or Shame?
Add up all the rounds and let's find out who the winner is!

Kids
Round One (+ bonus points):
Round Two (+ bonus points):
Bonus round:
Total:

Parents
Round One (+ bonus points):
Round Two (+ bonus points):
Bonus round:
Total:

Write your names where they belong. Will it be the Family Hall of Fame, or the embarrassing Family Hall of Shame? See pages 174 and 175.

game nineteen

only two games to go. don't forget to
add bonus points if you get all five questions
correct in rounds one or two.

Kids - Round One

Parents, it's another game and another five questions for the kids.
Let's find out how smart they are.

1	If you are 'using your noodle', what are you using?	☐
2	What is the shortest month of the year?	☐
3	What does it mean if you are 'nocturnal'?	☐
4	When the moon blocks out the sun, what is it called?	☐
5	Which is the biggest state in the U.S.A.?	☐

☑ for correct answer, ☒ for wrong answer.

SCORE:

Answers: 1) Your brain 2) February 3) You are active at night, and sleep during the day 4) A solar eclipse 5) Alaska

Parents - Round One

Kids, here's the first five questions for the parents. 1 point for each correct answer and 2 bonus points if they get them all right.

1	What is the nutrient in carrots that helps you see better?	☐
2	Which country consumes the most mustard every year: Germany, the U.S. or France?	☐
3	What's the name of Batman's butler?	☐
4	What country in the world contains the most islands?	☐
5	Who is automatically your first friend on 'Myspace'?	☐

☑ for correct answer, ☒ for wrong answer.

SCORE:

Answers: 1) Beta-carotene 2) The U.S. 3) Alfred 4) Indonesia 5) Tom

Kids - Round Two

Take it away, parents, with the next five questions for the kids. 1 point for every correct answer and 2 bonus points for a perfect round.

1	On which side of the plate should the fork be set?	☐
2	Finish this: 'One small step for man ...'	☐
3	What is 'Old Faithful'?	☐
4	What were the names of the 'Wright Brothers'?	☐
5	How many cents in $19.34?	☐

☑ for correct answer, ☒ for wrong answer.

SCORE:

Parents - Round Two

Kids, let's take it away with another five questions for the parents. There's 7 points up for grabs, so start asking!

1	Which character is famous for eating icecream, a pickle, Swiss cheese, and more?	☐
2	Which dinosaur name means 'king of the tyrant reptiles'?	☐
3	Where does My Little Pony live?	☐
4	Name the pizza which folds over in the half-moon shape?	☐
5	For what crime was Marie Antoinette beheaded in 1793?	☐

☑ for correct answer, ☒ for wrong answer.

SCORE:

Answers: 1) The Very Hungry Caterpillar 2) Tyrannosaurus Rex 3) Ponyville 4) Calzone 5) Treason

Kids - Bonus Round

Okay, parents, here's five bonus questions for the kids.
They'll score 3 points for every correct answer.

1	What did Roman emperors wear?	☐
2	Who were Moe, Larry and Curly?	☐
3	What is traded on Wall Street?	☐
4	What does a barber do?	☐
5	What type of creature is 'Flipper'?	☐

☑ for correct answer, ☒ for wrong answer.

SCORE:

Answers: 1) Togas 2) The Three Stooges 3) Shares and stocks 4) Cuts men's hair 5) A dolphin

Parents - Bonus Round

Only five questions to go and the last chance for the parents to improve their score. Take it away, kids!

1	Who were the brothers who wrote 'Hansel and Gretel' and 'Cinderella'?	☐
2	Where is the Haleakala volcano?	☐
3	In what mountain range is Mt. Everest?	☐
4	When were the Winter Olympics held in Sarajevo: '74, '84 or '94?	☐
5	What astrological sign are you if you were born during the last week of February?	☐

☑ for correct answer, ☒ for wrong answer.

SCORE:

Answers: 1) The Brothers Grimm 2) Maui 3) The Himalayas 4) 1984 5) Pisces

Game Nineteen - Total

Who will be inducted into the Family Hall of Fame or Shame?
Add up all the rounds and let's find out who the winner is!

Kids	Parents
Round One (+ bonus points):	Round One (+ bonus points):
Round Two (+ bonus points):	Round Two (+ bonus points):
Bonus round:	Bonus round:
Total:	Total:

Write your names where they belong. Will it be the Family Hall of Fame, or the embarrassing Family Hall of Shame? See pages 174 and 175.

game twenty

Here comes game twenty and this is
your last chance to add your name to
the Family Hall of Fame!

Kids - Round One

Here we go again with five questions for the kids. A maximum of 7 points is up for grabs if the kids manage a perfect round, so ask away, parents.

1	Finish this: 'Go ahead, make my … '	☐
2	Who lives in the White House?	☐
3	What is the colored part of your eye called?	☐
4	Who says: 'You're despicable'?	☐
5	What is a crop circle?	☐

☑ for correct answer, ☒ for wrong answer.

SCORE:

Answers: 1) Day 2) The President 3) The iris 4) Daffy Duck 5) The mysterious patterns that sometimes appear in wheat fields

Parents - Round One

Kids, here's five questions for the parents. Let's see how smart they are.

1	What color is a lobster's blood?	☐
2	What do kids in Holland do on the night of Dec. 6th?	☐
3	Name of the dominant male dog in a litter of pups?	☐
4	What gift is given on the 8th day of Christmas?	☐
5	In 'Peanuts', what is the name of Linus' little brother?	☐

☑ for correct answer, ☒ for wrong answer.

SCORE:

Answers: 1) It's clear 2) Leave out their shoes for St. Nicholas to fill 3) The Alpha Male 4) Eight maids a-milking 5)

Kids - Round Two

Parents, it's your turn to ask the kids another five questions.
Let's see how they go this round. Take it away!

1	What fruit is used to make most wine?	☐
2	What type of food is a tomato?	☐
3	Who uses a crystal ball: a jeweller, billiards player or fortune teller?	☐
4	What country does goulash come from?	☐
5	What country does the Loch Ness Monster supposedly live in?	☐

☑ for correct answer, ☒ for wrong answer.

SCORE:

Answers: 1) Grapes 2) A fruit 3) A fortune teller 4) Hungary 5) Scotland

Parents - Round Two

Five questions down and here's another five for the kids to ask the parents. Let's see how they go in this round.

1	If Bert were to 'friend' Ernie, what would he be doing?	☐
2	How do you say 'thank you' in Japanese?	☐
3	Which is NOT an Olympic summer event: equestrian, badminton, table tennis or bowling?	☐
4	What birthday did Barbie celebrate in 1988?	☐
5	In what county in England is Stonehenge?	☐

☑ for correct answer, ☒ for wrong answer.

SCORE:

Kids - Bonus Round

It's make or break time with these five bonus questions for the kids. Parents, take it away!

1	What would you do with gelato: eat it, wear it or play in it?	☐
2	How many days in a leap year?	☐
3	What kind of animation is 'Shrek': 2-D or 3-D?	☐
4	What can be worn to help you see more clearly?	☐
5	Where do men wear handlebars?	☐

☑ for correct answer, ☒ for wrong answer.

SCORE:

Answers: 1) Eat it – it's ice cream 2) 366 3) 3-D 4) Glasses or contact lenses 5) On their face - it's a moustache!

Parents - Bonus Round

Kids, here's five bonus questions to ask the parents. Each correct answer is worth 3 points. Let's see how they go!

1	Which national flag features a big, red maple leaf?	☐
2	What type of creature is the endangered gelada?	☐
3	What is a group of ants called?	☐
4	What famous character did Willard Scott create?	☐
5	Name the villain in the Wallace & Gromit film, 'The Wrong Trousers.'	☐

☑ for correct answer, ☒ for wrong answer.

SCORE:

Answers: 1) Canada 2) A baboon 3) A colony 4) Ronald McDonald 5) Feathers McGraw

Game Twenty - Total

Who will be inducted into the Family Hall of Fame or Shame?
Add up all the rounds and let's find out who the winner is!

Kids	Parents
Round One (+ bonus points):	Round One (+ bonus points):
Round Two (+ bonus points):	Round Two (+ bonus points):
Bonus round:	Bonus round:
Total:	Total:

Write your names where they belong. Will it be the Family Hall of Fame,
or the embarrassing Family Hall of Shame? See pages 174 and 175.

Notes

Notes

Notes

Notes

Notes

Notes

Notes

Family Hall of Fame

There's only one way you've ended up here: You won a game and showed the family who's boss. Congratulations and welcome to the Family Hall of Fame.

NAME:	SCORE:	NAME:	SCORE:

Family Hall of Shame

So, you managed to make it into the Family Hall of Shame. Not the best outcome, but cheer up - you probably scored better than the family pet!

NAME:	SCORE:	NAME:	SCORE: